ORBS VETUS

A Merline(
l'ono piacevole
le letture...

25/04/2015

CITIES SERIES 4

 Canada Council **Conseil des Arts**
for the Arts **du Canada**

Guernica Editions Inc. acknowledges the support
of the Canada Council for the Arts.

WILLIAM ANSELMI

ORVIETO

URBS VETUS

GUERNICA
TORONTO — BUFFALO — CHICAGO — LANCASTER (U.K.)
2009

Antonio D'Alfonso, editor
Guernica Editions Inc.
P.O. Box 117, Station P, Toronto (ON), Canada M5S 2S6
2250 Military Road, Tonawanda, N.Y. 14150-6000 U.S.A.

Distributors:
University of Toronto Press Distribution,
5201 Dufferin Street, Toronto (ON), Canada M3H 5T8

Gazelle Book Services, White Cross Mills, High Town,
Lancaster LA1 4XS U.K.

Independent Publishers Group,
814 N. Franklin Street, Chicago, Il. 60610 U.S.A.

Typesetting by Selina.
First edition.
Printed in Canada.
Legal Deposit — Fourth Quarter
Library of Congress Catalog Card Number: 2007929813
Library and Archives Canada Cataloguing in Publication
Anselmi, William
Orvieto : urbs vetus / William Anselmi. – 1st ed.
(Cities series ; 4)
ISBN 978-1-55071-275-9
1. Orvieto (Italy) – Description and travel.
2. Anselmi, William – Travel – Orvieto.
I. Title. II. Series: Cities series (Toronto, Ont.) ; 4
DG975.O7A58 2007   945'.652   C2007-903559-0

ORVIETO

URBS VETUS

Angela, Ezio – 1957 . . .

Gaze down, swooping towards Orvieto

From a distance, and under the Gemini sun, Orvieto is a narrative, an island written in the tuff. In the tuff, names, work, heroes and failures are entwined like the vines of a dream. There is no respite in the Umbrian valley that surrounds it, everything is a reflection. Only February with its fog licking its way through the lines of a face can still the lips, and suddenly time is inconsequential.

Yet to turn away would it not take away from each bitten cherry a few seconds, from each burst of juices the pulp of a story? Would you not want to stop, high on the hill past the cemetery, and consider how human flight becomes a leap of wrath in front of you?

Stand there. Orvieto is straight ahead in the air. Each curve of the road, descending for kilometers, until a temporary level is reached, just past the cypresses and the tombs, ascending, curve after curve, left and right, until the city door is trespassed: breath of asphalt then apnea. Stand there, Orvieto is in the distance. Breathe, calmly.

There stands Orvieto in the distance. Who is flying today, here, from La Rupe?

Delightful Gianna. Overhead a plane, silver hyphen glittering against the sparse clouds. No cosy traveller, harbour of an elsewhere, will be able to recount Gianna's flight trajectory today. Perhaps Luca Signorelli will, but he has her commodiously atop an infernal being, with the wings of a bat and horns of a goat. She is stuck in the Call of the Elect's final, painful depiction. Notice how Hell is reflected in his sardonic gaze, as he holds his place above the damned souls.

Here goes Gianna, throwing herself over the short tuff wall. See her crush in a confusion of bones near the paved road. Hardly aesthetic, the little fleshy puddles against the overwhelming grey of a road bound by yellow lines. She is not the last of a long sequence in the Malediction of the Tuff. The body of this sixteen year old, comical in its reach is invisible. Flying has this magic: it hides the points of a compass with a sweeping motion. No tree or bush is harmed in this flight. No taste altered or farmed.

Later, the gravel, the grass and the sullen gods will quickly absorb the shadow there. A dash of rain will complete the task so that others might follow, so that one more Icarus will point to the sky and substitute the sun by twist of arm. Give me honey and wax, baby.

Everything is still. Everyone is asleep tonight. No tippy toes will do, no breath withheld, no dull tongue, no candle. Fangs: to sink as fast as the wink of the inner eye. The pulse slowly skips a beat. Orvieto is a sea of lights. No moon atop the concave stop. Each eye dazzled by an inner glow. Ghosts go jumping in the flow.

Once, a generation ago, fireflies flew about.

Then came pesticides, fertilizers, industry. An increment in production for tilling the land made the peasants richer.

Red poppies. During an epochal change some god with a degree in botanical aesthetics decided to lavish them around like pennies from earth. Against the coppery tuff burning its surfaces away, the simple poppy became a strategy of beauty. It reflected the scope of the peoples that worked their way to this holy place. They came from the East, setting their traces on the volcanic spew hardened by the sun. The first settlement named by the Etruscans. Undecipherable words made the space on the hill a point of economic and religious power. All sanctified in June. The month when the linden trees explode outwards, each cluster, each fist a mesmerizing planet. The nostrils: tongues, fingertips. They reached the iron chord – the single iron chord taut as a bee drawing the poppy out from its sunset that connects the church of San Francesco to Il Duomo.

Palombella time. Everybody look out and look up and look around. Who is smiling? Let the service begin. Let the benign god, the single god, now, without any mating on the horizon, only a swift, simple sacrifice to make amends, bid you entrance. Bye, bye, dove. Let the mechanical apparatus carry your swift descent towards the treasure of mosaics. Scattered, encased between the stones laid down on the piazza surrounding the cathedral. Façades live on. The holy Rose, the apostles, the all-Beginning carved in marble.

Dove, we left you at the start in flight. Let's go back with a wink. You are free. As fast as an ear can hear, you are the little flame. Illumination. Descent among the crowd. The worship. You must survive the good auspices, the summer solstice. But among the children, sweating it out in shorts, shirts and tight suspenders, the cage is aflame. You are burning up, dove, at the shoulders. Burnt, a corposant in the air. Painful as a sunburn, as taut as eardrums afire. As light as a face alight with stupor. Next year the seasons will be dancing to this tune: Sputnik. Dove, Laika, a sacrifice of the wordly orbit, here, where the world has its center. Orvieto.

Via Volsinii, 3 – 1963

When Kennedy is shot, my grandmother is trying to barge into our home. She crushes the door wide open with her right shoulder. The key doesn't work, but the pea-green door is a softy. One, two and three small pushes and she is in. I'm five times as many full moons old. I'm wondering deep in the recesses of my mind if my nonna and I could not be Batman and Robin. She is stocky, about a meter and a half of solid peasant stock; me, I'm barely an Umbrian elf.

Inside, she tells me it is going to rain tonight. How does she know it? Time-tested, peasant knowledge of the state of things. The clouds outside are gathered like sheep.

It turns out the rain is more a storm than a blessing. Thunders and lightning, the streets quickly empty in the afternoon.

By evening, I drop a paper-made ship, the only *origami* I know, from the window. Will it float? It flies away, swept up by a rancid eddy.

Nighttimes like these give me the creeps, although Priscilla, my lover of a cat, keeps me warm, purring on my stomach.

It's one, long night. The full moon should be out. The right combination for the local werewolf to roam the streets. Nonna is full of old-times stories. The one about the *lupo mannaro* will haunt me through my family's stay in Libya.

He was just a man in his fifties, huge and strong, mentally challenged from god knows when, where, or what. Still, he played his role specklessly. When it was not raining, he would yell, trash things about, run around the square – a jogger before his time – and put his head under the cold water-fountain beside the piazza at night. I think his old mother would only let him out when the full moon showed around. The lunar, the terrestrial.

I would curiously pass by his house during the day. He was always at the window, talking to himself, burning away under the Etruscan sun. By this time I have read (image-reading, I couldn't read at this age, my uncle couldn't keep up with my fanciful explanations for the pictures and clouds that swam around my pupils) too many American comic books, seeing life through my imagined sense of being. I am alone, I'm an only child.

In my mother's house: Piazza San Giovenale, 12. Just about fifteen meters away from my grand-mother's home. My mother and I have just returned from la Palombella. My father is away. The displaced mechanic is working his life away at Ladispoli, near Rome. Orvieto is home to the ghastly orgy-porgy of the Corpus Domini. I am scared, a brown snail and a shell, antennae retreated inwards. Every explosion of the fire-crackers has made me cringe inside my bones, but my muscles are still twitching about. Urbs Vetus, the Old City, stands on an earthquake zone. I am the child of this environment. Throwing the suspenders (I will grow old hating those things), I go and hide. Where? In this house – second floor up. Windows facing the square. As large as an Old West fort. I'm a cowboy in the early afternoon. There is a secure place all for me. It's a little, fantastic, encasement in the wall in what we use as a depository room.

We have urns, huge sunburnt urns full of olive oil.

Big Etruscan ships, sail up the vertical river of hunger. I'm the Admiral. Space. A water basin where my mother goes washing fruit and veggies through the winter, and my face with cold water before bedtime. I am able to detect, rooms apart, through the kitchen, the bedroom walls, the fennel we are about to eat. I grow up with a reputation for detecting subtle strings of flora. Too bad I will develop some kind of allergy. It took me no time at all, in Nova Scotia, to free my nose from the violence of returns.

Orvieto, looking up

You, dove, the robin I could have been, a swallow scared of the Corpus Domini turnout. It is always a question of flying through the crowd. No sense in crushing against the cathedral in this early summer anticipation. Everybody is sweating. There are puddles and rivulets of wax and honey and salt and water stuffed in shirts' wrinkles and bloated ties that surround in trepid wait Il Duomo. Eyes as fixed as tuff-nails; eyebrows arched as paintings. We are bringing home a good omen. The depiction of a flying devil, horns and wings and all, atop a savvy blonde. When I take a picture, where am I? Where am I?

You are here. The arrow puts you squarely in front of a flying teenager deciding how she is going to leap. Is she going to pursue the wings hidden in her ribcage? Is she going to burst through the crowd? Is she going to finally sing? Yes, because she always had wings, a decoration in Etruscan times. Once the place and plan were settled, the religious engineers came out of the religious chambers and religiously decreed: this is the softest of all landings. Eons away from a fountain, just near the crash, this is where we land. Everybody comes running. The sun is atop the Etruscan tombs without a spark of dark, as you go flying through and through.

Corso Cavour – 1980

Sveglia! Your writing in flight is repose to the air chambers of the cypress wood. No tuff tablets about. Wood rots faster than a swollen kiss.

Brand their brains with this. Descend. Empty at the hands.

They sat you down, one summer evening, on the steps leading to the church in Piazza della Repubblica. *Piazza, bella piazza.*

Orvieto is older than Rome. What blood ties there were to the Etruscans are now this vinegar singed by a sheaf of impotent sinews. Banned from public space. You keep on laughing and crying, unaware. This is friendship they offer, a communal network of politically engaged new subjectivities. Movimento 1977, urbsvetus style. Banned, and you go flying, laughing.

Overhead, an airplane has already started its descent towards Rome's Fiumicino Airport. Hitting air pockets, it's a silver arrow softly drumming in the sunset.

Orvieto, the flipper priest tilts, abruptly, the first desiring machine, 1979

A syringe is an act of forgiveness. Always. The hand trembles, heroin is each ending nerve love-twisted. A needle, all previous damage comes undone. Everybone be happy. Zen moment.

Chiara is the first to leap, overdose number one in town. How many poppies are left before June?

Something has changed. To find poppies anytime you go to pictures. In the field seeded with grain, hard grain, the right hand is sufficient to collect in the dark room all the reds available.

Umbria is the green heart of Italy. Umbria is also one of Italy's three red regions. If you breathe right, you think positive, turn left as you can summarize it. Emilia-Romagna, Toscana, and smack center, no sea about, Umbria. The natives are red, red is their tongue, red the lungs, red the heart.

Tourists step out of a bus and are overwhelmed by the Duomo. One syllabic utterance.

They are polyester clowns. Some will never be able to enter the cathedral, no shorts allowed, that's bad taste, and will linger about on the grey-stoned stage around the first example of Gothic-Byzantine art snapping pictures aplenty.

Then comes the tourist, the avenger with a hammer, smashing the base marble carvings that depict Creation, at the bottom of the façade, consumption Stendhal style.

Late, at the sixtieth of the hour

A unruly tribe of seven-to-ten-year-olds claim one space where to play soccer. It's on this grey stage, the cathedral, an attractor point. The Cardinal's abode. An immense square that surrounds the Duomo. Seven steps up, a stage of stairs lifts you to the final platform. Two on the left, three in front, one on the right. There is also a meadow on the right. Play soccer there, you say? You deal with the slope. A slant is a slant is a ball that keeps rolling right, on a free fall towards the museum adjacent. And if the ball goes through the bars, who is to retrieve it? The museum has been closed since the time we were not yet born.

A ball, fifty cents worth, changes the world from ennui to a story told over and over. We are playing, late afternoon when the clouds have passed this way. May, the Virgin's month, the month of red roses. Inside the cathedral, old ladies play solitaire with a blackened rosary. A few tourists get high on the incense. The lonely widower eyes about, distraught by noise. The sexton, Frankestein's creation, appears suddenly out of the huge brown doors with spikes around the frames. Surprise, surprise, the balls ends in his hands. Sudden-death overtime. Us or him? Massimino the fox, steps forward, pleading. No more banging the ball against the church's door, no more banging away during the Virgin's functions. Mercy, *mea maxima culpa*. Full respect, amen. Please, give us the ball if you please. We bow down, we bow about, we bow without any clout. *Kirie Eleyson*. We, the children of proud working families.

We have all been an altar boy once. We have all been eyed, softly, hungrily by old widows upon our reading from the Holy Scriptures. We have all died in their mouths, those hungry, foul caverns of love. Holding the little bronze plate under their chins. Who will ever undo the wanton looks, the silly smiles, the *ekstasis*? How they were stolen away from themselves *ad illo tepore*. A simple white wafer, then Love for all. All you need is love, after all.

Santa Caterina da Siena was a simple child in comparison. No need to destroy the body. There is an easier martyrdom. Look up with trembling eyes to the altar boy, for he possesses the beauty of innocence. No need to read in the Altar Boy's Guide (*Guida del Chierichetto*, 1967) – freely provided by the congregation. Our brief appearance behind the altar, bell at hand, waking the nun from her early morning snooze, in San Giovenale: 7:40 am.

San Giovenale's early time

Orvieto's first church. San Giovenale's church is erected about one thousand and one hundred years ago. Some people talk about time in movies, mixing the appeal of war with things to come. Some things stand still, undisturbed from an irrevocable past. Some of the paintings have gone the way of the poppy, some still blissfully alight. San Giovenale is in the oldest part of Orvieto. It faces the hill where the cypresses bar each soul from hiding about: the chilly song of cats in love denied any resonances.

The chubby sexton is a heart of respite. Trust, whom shall you trust if you too believe? Simplicity is a technique of survival. Once the ball has purred against our feet again, the huge, brown doors close gently on our blissful world. There is nothing else left to do. Massimino takes the ball. The beauty of à penalty shot. Boom. Not like the persisting echo inside which has made sure, no malediction given, that Italy loses time and again a world cup. The Virgin Mary must have had a snaking fit before surrendering to the beauty of innocence. We ran away from Il Duomo placated and vindicated. For once, all the buried Popes could not restrain the fury of the sods of clay.

Tourists are still clutching their American portable banks. Seven o'clock. What punctuality. Do you think we will surrender it to Policeman Bocchino? Although we know the theory, no one has an inkling of practice. Outrunning him is not just a solution, but a resolve. He will never catch us, until the band of bandidos (we grew up on more comic books than Uncle Sam) disbands for good: June 14, 1969. Not soon enough. A little later mankind will lay claim to the Moon. A round silver ball.

Blues of the old world, we should have remained Umbrian, Etruscan.

Il Duomo: before entering, dip your hand

It doesn't matter the time of day or night. The flight of stairs around the cathedral is a free sitting zone.

Love among the ruins. The cart selling pumpkin seeds, licorice, *gassosa,* chinotto and postcards, is at the corner, on the hospital side. On your right, if you are squinting at the façade. Yes, where the slanted field of green is.

Cigarette butts float burning on the heart of each stone, each *sanpietrino*. Discarded seeds-skins quiver in the heat. What are they talking about? The guy with the Lucio Battisti afro, Peppe, is practicing English with Ruby from London. Quick hand gestures, beat of anedoctes out of this late afternoon. Swallows are making love beneath the blue-pierced strewn-sky. You get satisfaction in their cries, the sudden bursts that make passing priests cringe and buzz away like flies. The façade aglow. Rejoice. They weren't stupid, those medieval architects. The position was quickly chosen, the Duomo would be splendor, the source of light in the valley, a sacred plane of marble upon the tuff. The architecture of a miracle when words can only flaw, enchant and mesmerize.

The mirror of your *sophìa*.

First came the heretics. The place must lend itself to whatever is a *scarto*. The *piega*, the fold, the wrinkles in the cloth that adorns the table set for supper. A stain of grace.

Before the world was set upon its frame, a small congregation of a religious-political sect, the *Fraticelli*, coming from different paths, converged on Orvieto. Hunted in their regions, as foxes are today in Albion – the Rock – most escaped with their lives and tongues, and found momentary repose in our midst. Welcomed, their industrious ways gave a spurt to the economics of the land around. They practiced solidarity, a convention of the destitutes. Others came, from as distant as the land of Normandy or Germany.

They became one with the local population, sharing, in actuality, an ancient need. No man to man superior, but a commune, independent, with as many creeds.

Pope Bonifacio sent the Holy Army to vanquish these subversive practices of the common, higher good. God had cried, sending famine throughout the land just south. So they came: a few knights, the well-paid Foreign Legion of old.

Slaughter. The night turned to blood until over three-thousand souls were freed from their fleshy seeds.

Once again, Ovieto was purified. A castle of sorts still stands, the Pope's castle, where in summer, the best of times, He would come to see with his eyes a pious population expiate its crimes.

Bolsena (Rest, oh weary mind) – 1215

The lake of Bolsena is rainwater that collects, millennium after millennium, in the mouth of the spent volcano. It is here that the priest from Bohemia stopped, celebrated mass and drew blood out of thin air. The wafer, broken during the most solemn of moments, dripped with blood on the cloth of the altar.

He recuperated his one belief without going first to Rome to talk things over with the Peter, the Stoner. No anecdote here, just a few drops.

The cloth is holier in the holy shrine.

Erected, the house was already there to welcome another *spot*. A shelter more than ten feet tall, an offering throughout the centuries. This, the red snap of transubstantiation. 12 kilometers away. A lighthouse, on top of the old city. The construction starts in the twelfth century.

Not too far is Montefiascone. Another medieval encasement in this texture of hills and valleys. A real body this texture, the body of an old person's skin wrinkled and cracked by the sun, chamfered by the *tramontana*. You can still see these bodies about. Fluids dry up, without a story to be heard. Dust, ochre. Alexandria burns each time, embraced by the fragrant arms of the cypress.

Mountain big-flask.•Medieval times were entertainment made human. The Bishop from some dry town sends a scout to trace a route towards Rome. A wine route. The wine-scout is to mark the word *Est* on each town's wall, by the arched gate. *Est* is the sign the wine here must be drunk. Montefiascone gets *Est Est Est!* With an exclamation mark at the end. The Bishop was never to see the Pope.

He drunk himself to death.

By the entrance, we always laid down and watched, 1969

Peppe looks like Paul the Beatle. That's the guy with the curls, just got smack, smooch, smack on the cheeks. Smooth guy, no doubt.

Ruby is leaving. The bus departs: destination Rome. Afternoon blues. Sniff. Doors open to the *afa* in the square. The heat rises, wave after wave, after bouncing on the stones. My friends and I are watching, dead man style, floating on the marble stage. Now that I know languages, I can translate from the past without exaggeration.

Exaggeration: the weapon of the poor.

The stones reverberate.

Our Madonna of Hope appears as an import. The perfect blonde. Azure top. A light, white mini. Pink, high heels; no opals on her feet. It's another bus: Americans. A ventail of mini-skirts, a spot or two of nuns and some old, lobstery plums. Peppe, tail wagging, is already at her mercy. They all pass by.

How does he do it? When we share smoke together and become friends, he tells us. He sings. They swoon. *Che storia!*

Inside the Duomo, meanwhile. A widow, the worst of all constellations. She sees them touch. She faints on the spot. Hits her head on the marble, the coma lasts a day short of a week, oh blessed Virgin Mary.

Miracle, miracle of miracles *est*, she is back by Sunday. In time for her the grand Mass, her return among the saved and the elected.

Entrances, 1966: the vast emptyness, the organ

Summer time.•The main door of the Duomo is left open. An abrupt cold inside. No time to name how many found faith again. Swallows fly about around the huge pillars that hold the dome. The organ plays on. Actually, the organ player is practicing.

The first thing to do is to go for the *argent de poche*. Somehow tourists have this positive activity they delve in. Each water container, Trevi Fountain or cracked pot is an instantaneous deposit of free liras.

Each lira deposited is me coming back. Massimino holds me up as I go for the first basin. My hand is a fishnet. "*Niente,*" in a whisper. We blow out votive candles, lit by the dead for the living. Quick cross across the chest. Superstition pays. Onward, my faithfuls. The fishing basin near the central door. Who's watching?

The sum of faith totals forty-five lira. Cornucopia. That's enough chewing-gum to be shared for a week. Or, being hungry anarchists, a full day's worth of pumpkin seeds and change to spare. We leave no peel behind, everything goes down, in the vortex, as vapour rises from the stones.

Back inside. The sexton, whale eyes of gloom, stands triumphant on his conical figure. The referee of our empty late afternoons. A few Latin words murmured in ecstatic transport. Someone should have scripted us for a comic strip. We spread out like the rose from a shotgun. He never catches us. What would he have done with anyone of us?

We can go back minutes later and everything is as always was, neutrally fine.•Terrestrial Paradise.

La Cappella del Signorelli, then and now

On your right, ladies and gentlemen. The square is all around. You see right in front of you the long perimeter of flat buildings, cut in the middle by San Francesco. The street named after the saint? Only he could stop a wolf with words. Today we use one sound, no harmony, no tune. Something between light and sound, the bullet.

On your left, just beside what used to be the hospital: there, that small *vicolo*. You know about Vico? You can purchase replicas of everything, even the unknown.

The two-eyed cyclops is long dead. He never wore his glasses. Drowned, in the Paglia River's eddies. About a meter and a half of dirty water, during a particularly mild summer. His swollen body going round and round, forty-five rpms, a hit-single: what did he sing under water?

Never got married, never a friend beside a glass. Obviously, another in the sequence of the Malediction of the Tuff. My glass of white Nettuno goes up to you, silent companion, as you spin in your impossible story.

The small bovine-faced sexton, glasses and high-pitched voice says: "Ticket please." I look in his eyes, there is not one story to be told.

Inside the chapel, where Signorelli reigns. Splurge of coins, the tourists have gone for the mechanics of the story. Each coin, a language. The useless telephone, a reassurance. I pay, I know now and forever. *Pecuniam solvo ergo sum.*

The story is quite simple. Fra Angelico got commissioned to do a series of paintings depicting the final days of Humanity. He asked to be paid by the litre. Orvieto. He got the boot after too many blurred lines. Luca Signorelli steps in. A novice, a man with a bold stroke. *Ecce homo!* He's already looking ahead, the Renaissance bodies are coming this way.

And rays of fire from heaven. Bodies resurrecting. Skeletons halfway from down below. Bones collecting flesh on the go. Modernity transpires. Grandiose, bloodied modernity. Full-bodied characters, eating their way out of the earth. And the colors – it's Carnival time. It's the sexual frenzy of the Holy Flesh. The flesh that, finally, breathes again after the idiotic stupor of death. It's the flesh that wants to eat up every inch of space, every crook and cranny like a malady of love. It's buttocks and chests and faces of marble. It's the complicity of sin. It's men and women, finally awake, looking at each other, for the first time since the apple fell on somebody's head. It's time! This is the gravity of sexual hunger. How those saintly commissioners approved of this is not a mystery to me. They were men of the communion of the flesh. They saw the mirror of their desires finally depicted. The Call of the Elect. Each body, an offering to the God made flesh. Today, under the umbrella of our puritanical economic system, each body is virtuality and sugar.

On your left, as you enter the chapel. Who is the man with blonde hair, dressed in a long dark robe? And what about the man beside him? Luca Signorelli gets to be his own signature. He adds in loving parody, his drunken master, Fra Angelico. What are they looking at? Across from them: Hell. He has tailored an eternal story out of his own vicissitudes. As he is painting away, his wife has a dubious affair. Flesh to flesh, ashes to ashes.

He depicts his wife, a blonde captured in flight, atop a horrific devil, frozen in the fear of eternal time. Ah, *maudit* poet of the flesh. The simple stroke of an eternal revenge. Be gone, charlatans.

The master is always at work. Pier Paolo Pasolini, a.k.a. Giotto, a.k.a. movie director, said something very simple about it in the last few frames of *Il Decameron. A cosa serve?*

Orvieto, May 1871

Reconfigured castles scurry about under the moonlight, hidden in the palm of your hand, the sea is a reservoir of possibilities. A storm of dreams. Mad swallows in your chest peck away at the frozen veins in the heart. Imagine: the full bodies of energy unknown. Arteries, a fistful of arteries, exploding against the sun. No, not the skeletons, idiot, or the lost, or the blind. The Rose again. Laughing lightly.

What do we know of the world? Suddenly, a wave covers up the map of all existences. The *Tsunami*, my dear friend. And we drown.

Rimbaud is writing to all of us. Each one picks out of his poem the love song that sings throughout his muscles. It's the commune, floating up our way.

My friends and I, grade one of the *Medie* – junior high school – go on strike. We, grade ones and twos, co-ordinated by the third grade, go down the streets singing: "Dubcek, Svoboda. Honor to the Che." The rhythm of things to come.

In our eyes, Ian Palach has not burnt away like each Buddhist monk in Vietnam. He is another Phoenix to breathe in, deeply, in our lungs, one more beat, a lasting beat. No compromise, *no paseran.*

Suddenly, we are joined by young and old, workers from the machine shops. From the anvil and hammer shops that forge the sea alight, fishermen of a new day. My father is proud, a smile of fortitude and sacrifice. And the peasants are flinting away at their scythes. It's their time too. We are not alone, never alone. Red and black flags go up, like fireworks. Time is ours, for the taking. We march. My arms are entwined with all the others. I'm mixing myself in with the actors from *Allonsonfan,* the Taviani brothers' film. It's a simple trick of tears. Good night, *Babylon,* good night, good night. *Esta noche no paseran, compañero.*

Orvieto, circa 450 BYT (Before your time)

For the Romans, the Etruscans were a problem. The Etruscan system – men and women and children – was devoted to the afterlife. The Etruscans saw life as a preparation. They were singing the same tune as the Egyptians.

Most disturbing was the role of Etruscan women. Women had power, like men. And dealt with the arts. Spent time adorning themselves, bathing in the words of a lost tongue. Ointments and words. Perfumes. Soft, delicate skins, and the resolve of a marching army. Why conquer, when life is beautiful? You can only be an idiot to wage war against your next of kin, or the caress of nature in your loins. After the conquest, the Romans made sure that Etruscan women were depicted as whores. Raped, pillaged and destroyed everything their bat's brain could sense. Period. The whole system was corrupt. That's a simple justification for an invasion. The Romans. The Fascists. No similitude, just the same stupid, grandiose offering: a multitude of caskets. The reconnaissance planes of Emptyness. The Empire imagined by a small sect of flying dogs. The hollow paws. The bastards. *Esta noche no paseran, compañero.*

Postilla

The well of San Patrizio is left abandoned by the Romans, once, decades later, they take possession of Volsinii. The ear of the earth of waters fills in with refuse, excrement, broken plates and earth. More earth will be added to this spot.

During the Renaissance times, Antonio da Sangallo the Younger, will be commissioned by Pope Clement VII to build a well in anticipation of a siege. It will be completed in 1547 by Simone Mosca, under the auspices of Peppe III (a.k.a., Alessandro Farnese). The well will be built upon the very spot, testimonial of an art still practiced centuries and centuries after Queen Turan.

That was another story. The story of the Etruscan and the Romans and Queen Turan who changed myth and history.

Again, a double flight of stairs, a double helix that never meets, will lead the people and their donkeys to a bountiful source of refreshing waters.

Urbs Vetus will lose its hegemony over the country side in this battle of confederated cities, and will slowly decline, becoming subservient to the Vatican Empire for a few centuries until Italy is proclaimed.

In the early 1950s, an American tourist, later made famous by a discovery in genetics, will be so taken by this, *il Pozzo di San Patrizio,* that he too will fall prey to an everlasting vision.

If the body be water, and the waters do meet, they start at first in the most recesses of such a miracle of organic being. Deep below the flesh and the blood, where the cells turn to their history to be split one by one in love, in an exchange of energy, the double-helix remains as tuff stairs still sustain the well today, DNA, the fabric and narrative of life. This too a legend, a recent legend, one that was passed on to me, today, as we read, by Angelo Selmi, retired admiral of the Italian navy, class of 1892.

Orvieto underground

Queen Turan, a seer of many qualities – before the Romans usurped that way of life – saw to it that caves be built under and around the Etruscan hill with a series of tunnels connecting them: an underground beehive of sorts. It was the right combination of an illuminated vision: the practical side dictated the domestication of boars that would provide excellent protein in the event of a possible siege; and the esoteric, for lack of a better word, part of this network, meanwhile, is still in dispute.

Of all discussions set to paper in the annals of the analyses of Orvieto's underground, it is better to draw out what the explorers first saw, and what today's paying tourist will be an eternal witness to. Just for the sake of clarification, you can buy a ticket to Orvieto Underground, should you happen to visit, from the small business just near the ex-Hospital. That's right, the one on the corner of the small *vicolo* connecting to a cobweb of small streets, the business selling tickets to the bus, to the *funicolare*, to the Etruscan museum, and an array of reproductions of Urbs Vetus through the ages and Rome squares, and small bronze-like replicas of the Shadow, a lithe figure of a child that, it is said, accompanied the passage into the unknown, once Etruscan eyes were spent.

Briefly, what the first explorers saw, after so many years, was a series of *piccionaie*, a series of holes in the tuff, which were meant for pigeons, something light to eat in case of a stressing siege. A medieval flour-grinder, for the bread to accompany the meal. And a lot of smaller caves, all interconnected, as old as the Etruscan. This points to the fact that the same spaces, under the hill, were utilized over and over again, over time. For example, in the medieval period, many passages to and from different houses were used to carry out secret raids, where one family would try to kill off another, like the Guelfi and the Ghibellini throughout all of Italy. That's because one family supported the Pope, and the other one didn't. Meanwhile, in Florence, they were developing football (soccer) as a way of resolving conflicts. Machiavelli, in *The Prince*, talks about the necessity for the writer to coach, we would say today, the Prince to show his virtue by educating his fellow yes-men to the proper slogans by which to inspire the multitudes. Language, the way we make the world speak our mind, is a reflection of itself. *Forza azzurri*, the vacuous cry of the army that almost erased from history any impudence of the different.

La passeggiata, Corso Cavour – 2001

From Piazza della Repubblica, up towards the Torre del Moro, then right towards Il Duomo, touchdown, and back.

A Moebius strip of good health practices: walking, sniffing, talking, touching, scratching, smoking, sneezing, socializing, ogling and immoderate self-love. Starting around six, it continues until suppertime, around eight.

Then the cobblestones become a desert, not as cold, and human sounds, technologically enhanced for a crisper picture stolen by the breeze from the open windows, carry the *Telegiornale*'s presence about, the News.

Those were the times, when, after every movie, we would sit ourselves down for a long, political debate. Smoking Nazionali, when you found them, quoting Marx in and out of context, Gramsci's role of the intellectual and Pasolini's passion for the human as a disappearing *soma*. We recited a lay *mea culpa*, when years later, *Private Salame* resurfaced as a *buffone*, in the azzurri's entourage, changing every line according to the new creed.

I'm not a hermetic, nor an anchorite. I go through the streets alone, anticipating the encounter. I stop. I say, "Hello, Hello!" At times, someone of my sex will embrace me, kiss my cheeks, take my arm and walk with me a little. We will stop on the steps of Il Duomo. He will tell me: "How good it is to see you after all these years. What have you been doing?"

Maurizio, the bronze time-keeper atop the bell tower near the Duomo, shades another slice off the hour remaining in our, the best of times. What a mechanical device, *quelle merveille*. Clap, clap. Maurizio provides the cadence, every fifteen minutes for our games, hide-and-seek, *tappini*, the Western saga, *buzzico rialto*, nations, *lo schiaffo del soldato*, war.

It stands as proud as Hermes atop the tower. A small bell, the minutes, a bigger bell, the hours, around him. A hammer in his hands, this wonderful, solid, bronze Peter Pan, the cone hat on his head to protect him from all elements, goes about his job, swinging in a simple beat of Time. The creation of a local artist of mechanics, a mathematical wizard by trade, who devised equations with a ruler, known only by his first name, Ezio, and his birth date, 1329. Ezio, born between Orvieto and the Cemetery, at Il Tamburino, the little drum, a small village still living. A distant relative of my father, so I was told.

When my newly-made friends, Giovanni and Luigi, ask me: "What does your father do?" second day, in grade one, I tell them he builds Time.

They laugh and I surrender. We are holding hands as we descend the steps of our elementary school, *Distaccamento*.

Our mothers, our grandmothers, are waiting outside the big green door. The school is set and will close between the Duomo and Piazza della Repubblica, in one of the side-streets.

We are a swarm of bees, dancing for the Queen. The janitor, a broom in her hands, is already sweeping morning away.

We start to walk back to Piazza della Repubblica. Walking, talking. You say good-bye, I say hello. Which is one and the same thing, in Italian. Ciao.

Hello, Doctor.

My doctor, since we moved to Orvieto Scalo. Just below, the enclave that once surrounded the Railway Station. Now, a richer, more dynamic community than Orvieto, up above. The angels' fall has made good these last few years. Still, who can afford a house up there?

He grabs my right arm. His grip is solid, friendly, unforgiving, not interrupting his dialogue with his friend. No harm for him to continue with me present.

We are biochemical, organic material, that's what we are. Ah, the solid, materiality of the Marxist. It refreshes through and through.

He is discussing the possibility we now have to live on for almost ever. Approaching his early eighties, I feel like kissing this man. Erudite, alive. For me, the conception of what every man should be. Master of one's profession and then more. The humanistic and the scientific background, a settlement of many layers of a human being.

He's about my size, slightly stockier, a comma curved since the last lesson. One of Italy's experts of the heart – the mechanism of disenchantment. The eyes are compensating the cool breeze with fire. Holding on to my arm, and to his friend's, he is the master of this political oratory. Interjects the proper *porco Dio*, as any atheist should, as a semicolon. Continues.

We have the power, the ability, the knowledge to grow older than this. As I am writing, I undo his scientific certainty with a lousy recall, a *reverie*. I'm asking my Physics teacher, the possibility that the six million dollar man will become a factuality. I fail both his courses, Physics and Calculus. There goes my dream of becoming a scientist. All those DNA strands left untouched, no possible recombination.

The doctor gets closer. His breath is on my face, warm, sustaining. Now we have hit jack-pot. The American way of life – *che schifo*. The clowns who think their system is holistic. That's where they go wrong. Each system, stochastic, leads to a fracture in its encounter with other systems. He's got me.

Each system tends to disappearance, replaced by another complex attribution of parallel systems. Not quite Hegel, but then it's not the end of history we are talking about. I tend to agree, we, the determined bio-materials of a self-sustaining process. Add to this energy, and we are off, not even looking back on pre-prepared foods. The pigs, the pigs. Orvieto is square-tight in the middle of the celebration of pork. When I say *Dio porco*, I'm celebrating. Nothing else.

In celebration, how life becomes another's. Even silence has a human attribute. God is most certainly a pig.

I touch his arm, and bid another encounter well.

Braciole di maiale ai ferri. Supper's waiting.

Bye, bye. Hello!

At the station, August 1982

Champions, champions, champions! The framework is a classic. Three times, television commentator Nando Martellini repeats the storic word.

Italy wins the Football World Cup for the third time in its history. Italy-Germany, 3 to 1. Improvisation against order, enlightment against method.

To celebrate we descend on to the Railway Station and hang around. The shortest route possible. The Funicular. It's still going on water. The first car fills its base with water which is really just a huge tank, Orvieto. The second waits below, Orvieto Scalo. Ingenuity, since the 1870s, and plenty of water available, of course. A system of pulleys uses the weight of the first to lift the second, meeting in the bifurcation, in the middle of the single, two hundred meter steep track. We wave to the joyful crowd in the other car.

Thanks to the explosion of the car market during the joyful 1980s and the last drags of the Armed Revolt, the funicular stops running a year later. Decaying amidst the nettle and the vipers, it's only at the end of the century that it starts running again. A complex electrical system replaces water.

"I want to hold your hand" is still working its older charm.

A few months before Peppe walks into the bar. Bent over, playing *flipper*, a familiar body. The curly, black hair, the body size, the shoes, the tight ass, it's *Scalognetta*. Little bad luck. The nickname sticks. Able to foretell anything that can go wrong, which it will. Scenting a little fun, *Scalognetta* goes up behind the guy and starts mounting the closest of friends. An unfamiliar face turns around, says: "Do we know each other?"

We watch Peppe – though he thinks he looks like Jagger – approach two younger German girls, fully aware of a common musical past, as they desembark from the Florence-Rome *diretto*. Orvieto is an obligatory halt. Football? *Nein, nein, bitte.* Still, the sense of hospitality prevails and the singer and myself, the only one with an extensive English vocabulary, make our trip backwards. Language is a virus in the making, to correct old Burroughs. Before going back up, our quartet stops by the Hotel near the funicular. The cheapest and less controlled of hotels. The old holder is an accentuated Xaviera Hollander, especially in the reds that adorn her face, crow's hair about, head, eyes, nose and armpits.

We go for wine in a small tavern near San Giovenale, cheap wine, discreet eyes, long tables, straw chairs and huge barrels of Orvieto. If you want, they will bring out dry, black-pepper sausages and crusty, homemade bread. They only have licence for wine, but if you are hungry, hospitality would be betrayed if no food were to make your stay a little pleasanter: comfort, that's all.

By a roundabout way we end up through the Confaloniera. On the northern side, a long *viale,* poplars on both sides. A good walk for the lungs, oxygenate before action. The coolest side of Orvieto, always breezy. And below, the valley's show, hills of sparse lights in the distance. Above, in complete darkness is the static orgy of stars. Making love amongst the Etruscan tombs, at the end of our *passeggiata,* near the Funicular, in Piazza Cahen. There is one moment of panic, when in the dark, Peppe slips out, yells, imagining he's falling off the cliff. We laugh him on, a little tipsy, yes?, and continue the semiotics of cultural exchanges.

Learn languages, travel the world.

At the station, the return: September 1978

Outside the bar, at the station. A slow, pleasant evening. No more collective for the raising of snails, a jackpot idea. Do you know what they go for by the kilo? Snails know nothing about borders. Slowly, and most assuredly, they make their way up and about, over the fence. And all the gold turns to streaks and streaks of silver, thin lines of freedom, leaving empty their plot.

My friends have changed since the year before. Paranoia abounds. Grapes and grapes of paranoia. Bacchus has gone off the bottle, the angels have ripped their wings, one by one. The Metropolitan Indians have buried the axe, no more smoke goes around, no more prairies to occupy. No more lemons to hold on, squeezing change out of each confrontation. As the gas disperses, there are too many lost comrades. In the Garden of Utopia, that young God, we believed was all of us, is but a spectacle for the Armed Struggle components to outdo each other, while the Inquisition smiles on and history is erased.

Look at this picture, I am an urban guerrilla as I am about to pass the ball, on the field of the Ippolito Scalzo high school. How old were you, *babbo*? Your age, your age full of fury and sounds.

Valerio has mystic visions. Leaves his Catholic group, *CL*, to join, intermittently, between visions of depression, our little bar community. God has left him stranded at a fork. Suicide is one option. The other is to walk, silently, over and over each small, sideway street, night and day. At least the body is healthy, but sarcasm doesn't cut it anymore. He comes by, sits beside us in silence. All he wants is a moment of respite from the claws ripping away at each ventricle, cutting the brain into thin strips of paper, *coriandoli*. Not much is said these strange days. A few jokes, but the moment that the Carabinieri, in their jeep, show up for a quick coffee, silence crushes on our teeth. One always stands beside the jeep, machine-gun at the ready. The other two, looking over and about, stand nervously at the counter. One hand ready, the holster open.

Somebody, as they depart, informs me that you can get twelve years just for saying the wrong thing. No appeal, no lawyer. It's a new law, part of the emergency package. What about all the documents? The poems, the manifestos, the duplicated copies of political analyses, of the debate about the coming Revolution? Burned, buried, hidden, thrown in the river, stupidly, but erased from history for sure. Are you mad? Twelve years just for a poem. It happens. Worse things happen to our larger community. You want to spend the rest of your life in the special prisons?

Documentation abounds for this period. How Italy became the indomitable West's laboratory for social control. The repression, the games played on the lives of hundreds of thousands.

Heroin is the best, flooding in from the South, via the Americas, in an exclusive collaboration of intents. Undo the political unrest. Changes will be filtered by any means necessary. Done. By 1983, sources present this fact: over 250,000 hooked. A few made their way back, handfuls.

Paseran, amigo, paseran.

Alberto's house, 1993

The typographer, the friend who will grow closer as he displaces himself, lives on an off-shoot of Piazza della Repubblica. On his wife's side, they have lived in this house since 1100.

What is it like, for those of us for whom history is a book of dates and anecdotes, to imagine this? Passing down, generation by generation, the same nest of tuff. To know that those steps had meaning for all the blood and nerves you carry, even for the recessive genes? To feel, at each step, part of an ancient, established rhythm? You run away, of course. You have finally come to realize that Orvieto is not just an island that captures time unto itself, to regurgitate it in the form of the parade of the Corpus Domini. Every year, in June. Bodies that fulfill the medieval costumes *déjà vu*. No, Orvieto is not, just, an island.

Orvieto is a well-honed trap. No matter the technological improvement. Let the new parking lot, the mobile steps, the elevators be compendium to this. The elimination of foreign traffic is a swell idea. Yes. There is no escape, no one way out, no Ariadne's golden thread, no invisible ink, no mystery. The body has grown on the tuff fumes, the malediction. The body writes itself out of the narrative, forging for itself many identities, many more names. More than the Medusa's gaze, a Trickster's old tricks. The pages come necessarily together. The only sail left. Patched together from the remnants of days past. The few who have touched us are swimming down the vortex, incessantly. A cigarette points out all the eddies in this mouthful of air.

When you finally taste the sea, the salt is already starting to neutralize the long, sedimented poisons under the skin. The sun slowly turns the *mozzarella* peel around, the body turns porous, tuff, and furiously as you have erupted so will you drown. Romantic remnants, *n'est-ce pas?*

The throat burns, it's the regurgitation again. The little valve that cannot close off the reflux anymore. Gasp, the humidity. What's better: salt or acid?

Resurrezioni, or how we learnt to count

A glass of wine. The swallows. The poppies and the linden trees. In the summer, a delightful breeze.

The end.

Il C.A.R. (Centro Addestramento Reclute)

Sailing along, until the end of the Confaloniera, or, if you are leaving by bus or car, passing by Piazza Cahen, and renouncing the Funicular, and Saint Patrick's well, you will see on your right, the

Etruscan tombs, on your left, before the curve that bids *ciao, ciao* is the C.A.R. Was is the better tense. For now, different rhythms, a concert space.

Every forty days, new recruits from all over Italy, would be gathered and trained in the sublime art of war.

Nerone, a lost soul, was the only recruit kicked out of the army in living memory. Destroying an army tank and other disciplinary problems meant he obtained what others dreamed of: unconditional discharge. The Italian Army lost a local genius.

In 1967, following the directives coming from South Africa, where Dr. Christiaan Barnard brought to completion the first human heart transplant, Nerone outdid the master. The first cat to live with a rabbit heart transplant. Trans-animal organ exchange. Today, we cultivate pigs for the possible experiment. Nerone was definitely ahead of his time. Now, he bums cigarettes, money, anything really. If, finally, the experiment failed, whose fault is it? Nerone operated under the most gruesome of circumstances. Lacking in the proper training, and without any help of sort, material and human, he tried the impossible. Why inscribe him in a little, meaningless legend, that will disappear in a generation or so, when he showed what today's azzurri cultivate unperturbed: initiative, deep resolve, vision of scope, ingenuity, *e chi più ne ha più ne metta.*

President Berlusconi, as the only holders of such a portentous event, which parallels your previous *discesa in campo*, we hereby propose for him a marble statue, a yearly pension, a place, food, wine in abundance until he should join the great in Hades, the misunderstood genii of past generations.

Orvieto, 4-7-2002. The undersigned.

Il C.A.R, the first book, 1974

The long marches, under the *solleone*, the Augustian murderous rays. Everything stops in August, be warned. Shops close. Doctors, workers, students, even the indigenous terrorist goes to the beach, the mountain, away in August. August, the month attributed to the most peaceful of Emperors. The soldiers march back and forth, learning the proper discipline. Were we so lucky. How to mount and dismount a rifle? How to sabotage a city? How to learn to read lips?

August 1974, we meet up with Ralph. Italo-American, a devout philosopher. He makes love, not war. He gets a choice most of his peers can only dream of. He can do military service either in Italy or in Vietnam. He comes to Italy, forgets to show up for the military visit. The military police shows up a day later, thirty days in jail, immediately.

Along the Corso we brush with Simonetta, Chiara and Peppe. My hair is to my shoulders, black curls. Another Marc Bolan, he mumbles as we touch against his group of recruits, nicely dressed in their brownish uniforms.

"Where you from?"

"Canada."

"Me, I'm from the States."

A common displacement, he turns out to be a joker, a very horny guy, an athlete, a hard drinker, a guitar player.

We end up on the steps of the Duomo, ending our drinking binge with a full bottle of cheap whiskey, 3000 lira. He tells us he is trying to make it into the Athlete's Group. They have it so easy. Out of the recruits turnover, every time a new bunch comes in, the best athletes are chosen for training for the Athletic Compound. They practice all day, running, playing soccer, tennis, basket, swimming for the whole twelve months the military service lasts. He is going swimming.

It's about ten-thirty. He's busying himself with Chiara's abundant breasts. Peppe is watching tonight, waiting for the right opportunity. Simonetta has her tongue in my ear. We have moved on to the grass on the slope. "I am supposed to be back at 10:00 pm."

Immediate detention. Forty days in the cooler. Another stain on the record. In other words, the rest of the year under drill, no easy way out, no swimming about.

What are you going to do? Go AWOL. Screw the military. Our imagination is not bound by leaps, just by movies recently seen.

I'm going to jump over the fence, hit the dormitory before eleven, the dormitory check-in time, and hope for the best. Of course, doing this he can get shot.

One moment we are necking, the other we are running to save a friend. (Ah, to be possessed by that youthful sprint again.) Equal time between Donald Duck and Bakunin.

Equal time between the flesh dancing madly with the fireflies and sleep.

The narcotic mixture that leaves old ages asunder.

We watch him make it over the fence. No shots are fired. No unecessary harm is done to our literary apparitions. Never see him again.

Simonetta, Chiara, Peppe and myself hitch-hike down. Another train to catch. At our back, the Etruscan tombs. The girls are in front. Simonetta is short, a voracious blonde, with the bluest of skirts and white panties. Chiara stands at her side, her breasts pleading, projecting. Peppe asks for a cigarette. The two of us go smoke beside a tree. Pimps of a five-minute drive.

Minutes later, a Lancia-Fulvia, expensive, sporty, gray, stops in a screech.

"Where are you going?"

"Orvieto Scalo."

"Come in."

"Wait – our friends."

In Italian there is a little expression that goes, *far buon gioco a cattiva sorte*. Basically, you play your best even if things go wrong. Tell that to our soccer stars. We too get in. It's crowded in the back, and the two guys from Rome don't mind us, they are still trying to score with words.

Only, after the first curve at 110 km, the whiskey says hello and good-bye at the same time. Obviously, not impressed by Jackie Icks in front.

They ended up cleaning everything. The smell must have lasted for a few weeks, and they never got more than that. The girls were now looking after me, human *pietàs*, and Peppe too.

By the time home was a floating bed, my grandma takes over. Spends the whole night *in bianco* with vinegar under my nose, trying to revive me.

The next morning, in a different psychological space, we still kissed, Simonetta and Chiara and Peppe, before their departure.

Vinegar was around me, following me, altering each morsel, for the next few days. Ah, the simple, peasant solutions to a much too-stressful world.

Bookstore, inside the Torre del Moro, 1985 and beyond

Bookstore keepers are a unique breed. They are always interested in something, although they tend to know everything else. This is true of Italy, well, maybe of Orvieto; it certainly applies in a small scale to Barba. On any subsequent visit back, the first welcoming phrase is: "I got you something you will be most interested in."

Ah, the beauty of the knower. To know, ahead of time, what your customer and friend wants. It usually is a neat pile of the most interesting books, from cinema to cultural anthropology. There is little time for discovery, when a silver plate awaits.

Much like scaling the inner steps of this tower *Torre del Moro*. Who's afraid of heights?

Barba introduces me to Luana, his *compagna* from Rome. They end up introducing me to a world of music, another dimension of political engagement and animated discussion. It's nice to be valued, to be heard and contested, the small dialectical process of exchanges. Barba will never accept what, for me, is a self-evident truth: Humanism starts with the *Divina commedia*, not after.

Looking around Orvieto from the top of the Tower del Moro is a panorama of the heart. Better still when, later, another time, December 1999, a unique spectacle is available. It's jazz time, *jass*. Umbria jazz is more than a legend now. From Mingus to Jarrett, they have all come this way.

Today, standing atop a cold, high noon encased by *la torre* marks the first time that down below Corso Cavour offers its cobblestones. What a change of perspectives, to see the veins of an organ brim with activity.

On it is a street-band from New Orleans.

You know the sequence: the leader with a baton of sorts, in his special dress. Following slightly behind, the brass players. And Afro-American music clashing through the street. People stand amused on the side. It's free.

We've come a long way.

The last available Cioran, *Exercises in Decomposition*, is another exercise of elegance. Language in the guise of Achille's shield, the unbounding of Name. Displacement as the act of forgiveness, human materiality reduced to its, uncalled for, scales.

Who needs the survivors' faze, that Chatwinesque collaborative effort, when the mind leaps in and out of any of those sedimentations, the aphorisms of no guarantee?

Barba is a friend that fills in the empty corners. Through him, *Dead Man* becomes a classic.

No, can't see it.

Westerns were a joy for my blue-jacket days. But now? You want me to see a western? No, period.

So we go to Rome, to the only cinema that shows movies in their original language. He's already seen the movie many times over.

Only *Nostalghia* gave me a more lasting high.

Don't ask questions, lest you be cannibalized. Machine city, William Blake.

The band is slowly disappearing through a side-street, the music still reverberates. The people below are back to their steps, in this chilly, sunny, winter day.

Looking around, there is Palazzo del Popolo, to the right of Corso Cavour. The meeting place for the governors of the city back when. To me, it's still Cinema Palazzo, and James Bond, Fanthomas, Spaghetti-westerns, then hardcore porns from Germany, to whet all appetites, and the Hardon Orvieto Club (HOC). We would sit in a group, providing a running, sport commentary for the isolated figures interspersed about the seats, get ready here comes Harry, the Talking mule, here comes Black Beauty. Then lights out.

Years later, a remodeled, restructured Palace of conventions welcomes all the little floods to this parody of an outfall, this drying puddle. My neurons go in a frenzy, bypassing all synapses, when the first post-Fascist meeting of *AN* takes place there. How could you? The direct descendants of *la Repubblica di Salò*.

Barba, who's by now a city councillor, accepts it as the exchange of the new political reality.

Blah!

Blah, when just a year before, in December, a gospel choir sings in playback, and people, who must be from Orvieto, join to dance in the aisles.

Liberation.

Blah, when the white choir leader yells out, repeatedly: USA.

Such human heights are giving me the sensation to follow this vertigo over the tuff wall.

Since grade one, the very first day of school, any height over four meters has held an inexplicable attraction for me to jump over it. It's not a suicidal impulse, just a running infatuation.

Fear attracts, pulling every limb in, every oar in. Then the little ship, in its solemn and only mute fury, no matter how calm the sea, has but one direction. The abyss opens up, clearing its way of previous wrecks, algae and mermaids, just this time.

Where's that ship, flyers of the Tuff?

I am sorry.

Time to retreat, ever so slowly.

Down the steps, always to the left, spiralling down comrades, steps to circle, stretch my morose brain into the shape of a porcupine. Back into the bookstore, the head a-spinning, a Marlboro quickly fixes itself to my peaceful fingers, crack of a match, my throat is a fury of black smoke.

Cazzo di contraddizioni. Argh.

Luana, her antennas sensing the built-up wrath, takes my hand. Let's go for coffee. I have a friend I want you to meet; we are supposed to meet at 12:30 in Montanucci's bar.

Manuela is waiting, it's another world.

Barba joins us shortly afterwards, he's closed early. Luana's eyes spark up. Spring is in the air, months down the road. The Shadow is hungry for love. No winter will stop his story short.

Time to eat, it's another world.

Time to disappear to another world.